MONEY POWER For Retirement

By Tama McAleese
Certified Financial Planner

THE CAREER PRESS
180 FIFTH AVE.
PO BOX 34
HAWTHORNE, NJ 07507
1-800-CAREER-1
201-427-0229 (OUTSIDE U.S.)
FAX: 201-427-2037

MONEY POWER For Retirement, ISBN 1-56414-051-2, $6.95

To order by mail, please include price as noted above, $2.50 handling per order, plus $1.00 for each book ordered. Send to: Career Press, 180 Fifth Ave., PO Box 34, Hawthorne, NJ 07507. Or call Toll-Free 1-800-CAREER-1 to order using your VISA or Mastercard or for information on all books available from The Career Press.

IMPORTANT: While much careful thought and depth of research have been devoted to the writing of this book, all content is to be viewed as general information only and should not be construed as actual legal, accounting or financial advice of a personal nature.

The ideas, suggestions and general concepts are subject to federal, state and local laws and statutes. The ever-changing economic, political and international environment may well demand re-interpretation of some or all of the concepts presented herein.

The reader is urged to consult competent legal, accounting and tax advisors regarding all legal and personal financial decisions. This book is not meant to be utilized as a substitute for their advice.

Library of Congress Cataloging-in-Publication Data

McAleese, Tama
   Money power for retirement / by Tama McAleese.
      p.   cm.
   Includes index.
   ISBN 1-56414-051-2 : $6.95
   1. Retirees--United States--Finance, Personal. 2. Retirement income--United States--Planning. 3. Retirement--United States --Planning.   I. Title.
HG179.M3739   1993
332.024'01--dc20   92-42044
                                       CIP

Table of Contents

MONEY POWER
For Retirement

Introduction

There's Still Time To Change Your Habits

Every morning in Africa, a gazelle wakes, knowing she must run fast that day or she will be killed and eaten. At the same time, the majestic lion awakens, knowing he too must run fast—faster than the gazelle—or he will eat nothing and eventually starve to death.

Whether you picture yourself as a proud lion racing confidently toward a comfortable retirement or a dainty gazelle, carefully picking your path through critical financial challenges, when that sun comes up on a brand new day, you had better be up and running.

Mistakes you're probably making

The most popular retirement plan in American today is winning the lottery. Or, as one commercial for a not-so-great investment option tells us, most Americans spend more time planning their two-week vacations than they do for the 15 or 20 years of retirement living.

Don't feel bad—most of you are probably making the same mistakes. And the good news is: You *can* correct them. Let's start by recognizing what the dozen most dangerous mistakes are:

1. *Failing to plan.* Consumers can easily plan how much underwear to take on a weekend getaway, but many procrastinators never get it together for the most serious phase of their lives, their retirement years. Though you will need to modify your goals and objectives as your life develops, you must start erecting a framework on which to build concrete and realistic solutions—*now*.

2. *Depending on others to take care of you.* Company pensions, Social Security and social insurance or entitlement programs may shrink drastically or completely disappear as funding pressures increase and the number of qualified entrants grows. *At least one third* of your total retirement income will need to come from personal savings or supplementary pension plans.

3. *Spending too much now.* I'll say it more than once in this book: There is no deep secret to building a secure retirement. If you spend everything today, you won't have enough for tomorrow. You need to seriously plan and save for the day when a regular paycheck is replaced by a fixed monthly pension check...or no check at all.

4. *Waiting too long to start saving.* If you start early, time can be your friend. The more time you have for your money to work, the fewer original seed dollars you will need to invest. The

magic of compound interest is truly the eighth wonder of the world.

5. ***Ignoring inflation.*** The erosion of purchasing power through inflation is the most deadly money-killer over time. It is also the primary reason so many of the elderly are in a financial pickle today.

   Inflation will not go away, and anyone planning to live for more than three years has to tackle it. Once its insidious symptoms appear, it's too late to protect yourself.

6. ***Putting retirement savings into "safe" and "guaranteed" investments.*** Most current retirees were told their money *must* be safe and guaranteed—you wouldn't want to lose principal, would you? Meanwhile, the large institutions that were telling them that (and in which, naturally, these retirees deposited their nest eggs) were investing in the very vehicles they were warning everybody about!

   Long-term money like your retirement savings must protect future purchasing power, and fixed-income investments have historically *not* kept pace with inflation and are *not* expected to do so in the future either. Some growth on your capital above inflation is a must.

   There *are* no "safe" investments. If you try too hard to avoid one type of risk, you will surely fall victim to another. Risk is everywhere; the trick is to learn how to manage it.

7. ***Retiring too early.*** Our current retirement system is not designed to let workers off the hook easily. Most programs, including company pensions, were meant to *supplement* other income for the few years between the normal date of retirement and death. Most retirees have little concept

of the total dollars they will spend during their last years.

This condition is exacerbated by early company buy-outs that encourage workers to leave. Many workers believe they can supplement their income through other employment but, unfortunately, often discover the hard truth: No one else wants them either.

If you are planning to retire early, you must get professional advice (*not* from a financial product vendor) and some realistic numbers to make sure that you are not likely to outlive your retirement savings.

8. ***Not setting up a monthly savings strategy.*** Most folks budget upside down: They pay themselves *last,* so they always end up with more month at the end of the money.

Pay yourself first with an automatic bi-weekly or monthly savings program by payroll deduction or through your checking account. If you don't see it, you won't spend it. And if you don't spend it, it will compound and grow.

When you retire, you should continue saving each month for as long as you can. Eventually, inflation will catch up with you, and your monthly income won't stretch as far as it should. Practice chipmunk economics while you can: Store away unused cash for the future.

9. ***Putting all your retirement eggs into one basket.*** Diversification is the key to both safety and the long-term accumulation of wealth. Don't put all your retirement savings into your company 401k or employee stock plan. Don't invest only in one *type* of investment such as bank CDs, insurance annuities or policies, stocks or even stock mutual funds.

Diversification reduces risk to principal. Municipal or nonprofit institutions often have retirement or deferred compensation plans with only one company. If that company should fold, how will you feed yourself for the rest of your life?

10. ***Eliminating your annual IRA contribution.*** After 1986, the immediate tax write-off you got for your IRA contributions was limited or completely excluded for some of you. Many consumers went back to spending the money they had previously saved. You are making an expensive mistake if you abandon your annual IRA account, ***even if you can't deduct any of it from today's taxes.***

You could be losing $50,000 or more without the tax shelter of tax-deferred earnings for the many years your money could be protected in an IRA account. Congress never lets any good deed go unpunished. Don't follow in their short-sighted footsteps.

11. ***Purchasing inferior investment vehicles.*** It's not what they *say* but what you *sign* that matters. In the thousands of financial contracts I have seen over the years, I have never seen the terms "fair" or "friendly." Every contract is drawn up by an attorney, one paid by your financial adversary, *not* you.

The bold print may giveth, but you can bet that the financial industry will include some fine print to taketh it away. Every salesperson has the same financial challenges of retirement you are now facing. The only way they can meet *their* goals is by sharing *your* money. Learn to read before you sign, and to compare before you purchase.

12. *Following traditions that didn't work then and won't work now.* The last generation was advised to do three things with their money: (1) purchase a home; (2) deposit money in banking institutions; and (3) send the remainder to insurance companies. None of those suggestions worked for *them*. They won't help you reach *your* goals, either.

Do you want to eke out your "golden years" on the measly Social Security stipend that Uncle Sam might not be able to deliver, given the woeful condition of our federal finances? Or do you want to live comfortably—golfing, vacationing, enjoying your hobbies, doing all of the things you wished you had time for while you were working for a living?

Most intelligent people certainly would opt for the latter option. But in order to do that, you had better start planning now. This book will tell you everything you need to know *now* to enjoy your retirement, to reward yourself for a lifetime of hard work.

Does this mean putting off all of the pleasures you'd like to have today, just so you can have a better tomorrow when you say good-bye to your co-workers for the last time? Certainly not.

Having a comfortable retirement requires only good planning, making a place in your weekly budget for modest savings that will produce a healthy nest egg and the right long-term investments that will help your savings avoid the ravages of inflation.

Reading this book will help you begin to construct the right framework for creating the plan that is exactly right for *you*.

Chapter One

Improving Your Retirement Planning I.Q.

Let's start with the bad news: If you are like most people, the amount of money you will have saved by the time you're ready to retire simply won't be enough to support any kind of existence we would normally refer to as a lifeSTYLE.

Without proper planning, your retirement savings are being ravaged by inflation. In fact, the $1,000 your parents put away in a nice, "safe" investment in 1955 has declined in buying power by nearly 80 percent.

And those corporate and union retirement plans some of you have been banking on are in rather shaky financial shape or even been wiped out by the takeover vultures of the '80s.

What's more, there is the uncertainty that clouds the future of that monthly stipend to which all working Americans are entitled at retirement: Social Security.

These sorry developments beg the question: Will you have enough money to live on at 65...and 10 or 20 or *more* years thereafter?

Now for the good news

And now the good news: Relax! While these problems certainly are vexing, they simply should not prevent you from enjoying a wonderful stretch of rocking-chair years.

There is no great mystery to retirement planning. If you burn up your monthly paycheck building an inflated lifestyle and saving little or nothing for the period when you really need it, you will inevitably wind up living beneath your needs later.

You must earmark some of your money for retirement savings and put together a smart combination of personal investments that work harder than inflation so that these hard-earned savings will not be eaten away. Like Alice in Wonderland, your money has to work faster and faster each year to keep you living at the same pace.

And you need to follow some very basic steps. While I will be discussing each of these in detail in succeeding chapters and have already touched on some in the Introduction, here are the key rules in a nutshell:

Inflation will never go away

You must plan to stay ahead of inflation or you will become its victim. While you may be tempted to invest all of your funds into bank or S&L CDs, savings accounts, insurance annuities and other fixed-income vehicles, you must always manage some of your assets for future growth.

When guaranteed investments seem to yield higher returns, underlying inflation pressures may be even higher. For example: 1980 bank CDs returned as much as 14%, but the prime lending rate was over 21%. In 1986, when CD rates staggered to 6%, inflation was only a whisper at 2%.

The *real* return on savings was better in 1986, even though the interest rate was eight points lower, because inflation was so much lower. Learn to do this "inflation math" so you know what you're really earning (or losing!) on your money.

There is no such thing as SAFE

By investing only in vehicles that are advertised as safe and guaranteed, you are programming yourself for failure to compete successfully against inflation. You are also guaranteeing the very losses you are so earnestly attempting to avoid: the loss of your principal through shrinking purchasing power.

No mutual fund, no stock, no bond, no CD is *safe*—all investments move up and down daily, including those inside banks and S&Ls, insurance companies and the U.S. Government. *Real* safety comes only through diversification, the kind that is taught in every chapter of this book.

Take control of your financial life

Most of your life, so-called experts warned you against managing your own money. So you gave it to the institutions who were busy mismanaging *theirs*. Make yourself your own portfolio manager; guide your *own* investment decisions without their help (and their fees).

Relinquishing your retirement funds to strangers may be akin to hiring the fox to guard your henhouse. The financial industry's major objectives are to create commissions, pay their expenses, and charge you fees, with your money as their asset base. If they mismanage funds, they always have you, the taxpayer, to bail them out. Where will you turn if they mismanage *your* money?

Create a budget...and stick to it

Retirement is the most critical phase of your life because you cannot increase or replace your income as you could when you were working. You need firm figures for expenses (outflow) and income. You also need a spending and savings plan for the day when your paycheck is replaced by a smaller fixed monthly pension, social insurance payments or, perhaps, no checks at all. With a financial map, you can tackle those long retirement goals with the confidence that your money will last as least as long as you do.

Replace worry with education

Fear is paralyzing, while a financial education will empower you. Information is more valuable than the money itself, because with the right information, the money will come. (In other words: Keep reading!)

Know how much your future will really cost

Ignorance is not bliss. Only when you understand how significantly inflation will erode your future can you adequately protect yourself. Financial planning is not just for the rich. The less money you have to work with, the more crucial your decisions will become.

Make an estate plan

Even the young should have a secure estate plan. A will, a durable power of attorney for management of your financial affairs in case of disability, and a medical will or health care power of attorney may be sufficient for your financial status and the manner in which your assets are titled.

Before you opt for more complex solutions, like a trust or estate planning insurance, weigh both sides of any proposal. Attorneys make money-creating trusts, and insurance agents receive large commissions on the sale of their products. Short-sighted solutions can create long-term consequences after your death.

Read, read, read...then read again

Financial products for retirees and the elderly are notorious for contradictory and deceptive language as well as limited or downright inferior benefits. Some agents prey upon the fear of the elderly, promising advantages not reinforced in the written contract.

Never purchase nursing home coverage, medical supplement policies or financial investments without first requesting and thoroughly reading a specimen contract. Get a second opinion from consumer magazines which do *not* solicit products themselves. Don't purchase products from consumer groups without comparing their benefits to alternatives. Many of these organizations receive *some* "cut" on the sales they solicit.

Ignore the salespitch and go right to the written word, your contract. Carefully read the sections marked exclusions, limitations and risks.

Quality long-term care insurance is *not* cheap

Avoid buying any kind of insurance policy primarily on price. A cheap premium could mean limited, inferior or excluded benefits. Throw away insurance offers solicited by mail or telemarketing.

Visit your library and request consumer magazines that evaluate insurance companies and their health products. Then call several companies and ask for a local agent and a specimen contract. When the agent calls you, explain that you will call them when you need assistance.

Compare one contract with another and ask uncomfortable questions of each agent you interview. Expect them to put the verbal promises they make during the passion of a potential sale in writing on company letterhead.

Beware of dread disease and accident policies

So-called dread disease policies—covering cancer or Alzheimer's disease, for example—offer relatively limited coverage. Why? Because no company that expects to make a profit on the sale of its policies would isolate the most dangerous health risks, then sell *broad* coverage to individuals at affordable prices.

With a major medical plan such as Medicare, your current company health insurance, or an individual catastrophic health insurance policy, one Medigap or broad supplemental health policy will suffice for extra protection. Specific treatments for particular diseases should be covered within the framework of a high quality major medical policy.

Use your common sense

No one will ever invest your money for nothing, and any such promises should set off alarms. If it sounds too good to be true, it probably is.

Never buy on the advice of others

Referrals are the most common source of financial product sales. Well-meaning friends, colleagues and family can damage your financial future as easily as any vested interest.

Think before prepaying death expenses

Folks are emotionally drawn toward funeral pre-need programs, and promises of a guaranteed price lead them to believe they will get something for nothing. The funeral director will invest your money no better through the years than you can, and you can't wring blood from a turnip (or extra costs out of funeral directors) if the investment capital does not match rising costs for their services.

There are other considerations: Where will that money be invested? Who will watch over it so it is not mismanaged or misspent? What if you move to another state and change your final plans? What will you do if the funeral home goes out of business or the owner dies before you do?

Most folks have homes and other assets that can be liquidated after their decease to pay for last expenses. I would rather the funeral director bill your estate than take dollars from you now, before you know if you will need them in the future. Make an informed decision before committing dollars sooner than you need to.

Review all life insurance policies

Your problem used to be dying too soon. Before too long, it may become living too long. If you are at or near retirement age, have few or no liabilities and no one depending on you financially, why do you still need death insurance? The agent may need an annual commission from your continuing premium payments, but you cannot afford to help anyone else create a secure retirement plan.

Sometimes insurance companies collect so much in premiums ahead of time that the policies are paid up when you retire. Some of these promises were built on higher dividend scales and those vanishing premiums may surface again in the future. But even if you no longer pay premiums to an insurance company, you have a healthy piece of cash locked up inside your policy. This money could instead be working for you.

If you have cash surrender values and assets which can be liquidated after your demise to pay your death expenses, free your dollars and use the money for your own benefit.

Never invest out of greed or fear

You must become a disciplined and cautious financial consumer. As government guarantees are stretched to cover more failing institutions, consumers may find themselves alone, without the protection they expected. So they'll frantically chase the highest bidder, forgetting that higher yields inevitably mean greater risk to investment principal.

Buy the steak, not the sizzle.

Before I discuss all of these topics—Social Security, Medicare, insurance, your pension, estate planning, etc.—in the following chapters, let's take a moment to test your retirement-planning know-how. This will help you figure out what areas you really need to educate yourself about.

So turn immediately to pp. 23 and 24 and Test Your Retirement I.Q. (No cheating—don't look at the answers or at other chapters in the book just yet.) Then come back to the section below to check your answers.

How did you do?

Here are the correct responses to the questions in our little test:

1. *False.* Conservation of *purchasing power* should rank as the primary objective of any retirement plan. Inflation is the deadliest money-killer over long periods of time and represents a *guaranteed* loss of principal, as dangerous as any other potential loss. It's not what you make on your money that counts, it's what you make above inflation that really matters.

Regardless of your age, you must achieve some growth on your investment portfolio. Fixed-income vehicles such as CDs, government bills, notes, bonds, corporate bonds and insurance fixed annuities alone will not outpace inflation over time.

Growth without undue risk should be your retirement investment objective.

2. *False.* If you are planning to live for more than three years after you retire, keeping pace with inflation is vital. Therefore, you must always manage some of your money for growth.

3. *False.* If you pay fewer taxes, you will be in a lower tax bracket. That may mean you are eating fewer meals per day because you are making less money than you need to meet the escalating costs of living.

4. *False.* The only bills that will stop are the mortgage on your home (assuming you didn't take on a 30-year mortgage when you were 40 or older) and the excruciating college tuition you might now pay. *Inflation* won't stop, even though your current income and raises *will,* replaced by a smaller monthly pension with little or no adjusted living increase.

Income, property, school and other federal, state, local and user taxes will continue to spiral upward. The cost of groceries, medical prescriptions, treatments and other services will also climb. Therefore, your cost of living might actually *increase*, not decrease, after retirement.

5. *False.* Everyone needs at least a simple estate plan, such as a will and appropriate ownership titles on their financial property.

6. *False.* Very little of the cost of nursing home care is picked up by Medicare. You might need a long-term-care policy or contingency plans for nursing care.

7. *False.* If your company becomes insolvent or moves south of the border, it might be able to terminate its pension liability and eliminate other current retirement benefits.

8. *False.* If your retirement pension is sold to an insurance company, the company can spin off its liability and avoid the regulatory eye of the Pension Benefit Guaranty Corporation (PBGC), the federal agency that guarantees workers' pensions.

9. *False.* Life insurance is designed to replace income for your family while you are young and their financial security is

at stake. Your major concern now should be living and maximizing every dollar for your own retirement needs.

10. *False.* Some organizations might be well-meaning yet understand little regarding the financial products they recommend. Others might receive some reimbursement for products they solicit. Perform your own research; never buy on the advice of others.

11. *False.* Quality is the most important criteria when purchasing any kind of catastrophic insurance, including health and long-term-care policies.

12. *False.* Such "dread disease" policies generally have mediocre or inferior benefits. Stick to a major medical health policy that covers all types of health problems, not just isolated conditions or illnesses.

13. *False.* This mistaken belief is the primary reason too many of the elderly currently live below the poverty line. Social insurance programs are designed to act only as supplements, not provide full retirement incomes.

14. *False.* Time is money, and compound interest is the eighth wonder of the world. The more time you have to compound your retirement funds, the fewer original investment dollars you will need. Assume your goal at age 65 is to accumulate a lump sum of $100,000, and you expect to earn 10% annually on all money you invest.

If you start saving at age 25, you will need to contribute only $16 per month. Wait until age 35, and you will need to contribute $44 per month. Waiting until age 45 will cost you $131 per month. If you hold off until age 55, you will be looking desperately around for $484 a month to invest.

By letting compound interest do most of the work, you can achieve your financial goals much more easily and with much less money...*if* you start saving NOW.

15. *False.* The long-term power of an IRA lies in the tax deferral that protects your earnings from current taxation until your retirement. You should contribute on an annual basis *even if you can't take an immediate tax write-off.*

16. *False.* Retirement years are getting longer as workers leave employment at earlier ages. Eventually, retirement might become one-third of your lifetime.

17. *False.* Only hospitalization is paid by Medicare. Medical expenses are paid by *you* directly or indirectly (taken out of your monthly Social Security payment).

18. *False.* Medicare does not kick in until your 65th birthday. Until then, you must rely on your employer's health program or an individually purchased health care plan.

19. *False.* Social Security cost-of-living adjustments are linked to the Consumer Price Index. They might *not* match the cost of goods and services you are purchasing. You *will* need supplemental income.

20. *False.* More employers are cutting benefits to retirees before government mandates force them to shoulder more responsibility for retired workers. Don't expect your retirement benefits tomorrow to be as good as they are today.

21. *False.* You have nothing better to do than to watch over your own retirement savings. You will take better care of your dollars and have a greater interest in maximizing them for your own benefit.

22. *Possibly False.* More often today, older children are moving back home (often with their *own* children) due to divorce, the death of a spouse or as a single parent with a child. Today's grown children are also waiting longer to marry and leave home.

23. *False.* Personal real estate, as we have soberly discovered, doesn't always increase in value. At best, it barely keeps pace with inflation. However, as home prices increase, so does the cost of living. With retirement funding, you must *outpace* inflation over the long haul. Therefore, you will *not* fund your retirement based principally on your home's appreciation.

24. *False.* If you save 10% of your income for retirement, you have 90% left over for living purposes. If you can't live comfortably on 90% of your income today, you are over-spending

and over-consuming. Saving and spending are *not* conflicting goals.

Saving is merely not spending today so you can spend more tomorrow.

Retirement planning means that you may indeed be able to have everything, though perhaps not right *now*.

Test Your Retirement I.Q.

True or False?

1. _____ Safety of principal should be the foundation of any retirement plan.

2. _____ During retirement, creating income should be my main objective.

3. _____ I will pay fewer taxes in my retirement years.

4. _____ My living expenses will go down after I retire.

5. _____ If I have few assets, I don't need an estate plan.

6. _____ Nursing home care will be paid by Medicare.

7. _____ My pension plan is guaranteed by my company.

8. _____ Retirement pensions are guaranteed by the U.S. Government.

9. _____ I need more life insurance now because I have more assets to protect.

10. _____ I should purchase financial products on the recommendations of consumer groups.

11. _____ When shopping for health care policies, price is the most important criteria.

12. _____ If Alzheimer's or cancer run in my family, I need special insurance for these risks.

13. _____ My company pension, Social Security and Medicare are all I need.

14. _____ I'm young—I have plenty of time to wait before I start retirement savings.

15. _____ I don't need an IRA if I can't deduct my annual contribution.

16. _____ Starting retirement savings at age 45 is soon enough.

17. _____ All Medicare benefits are provided free from the government.

18. _____ Medicare will take over as soon as I retire.

19. _____ Social Security payments will keep up with inflation.

20. _____ My company's health benefits are guaranteed in retirement.

21. _____ Professionals can manage my retirement funds better than I.

22. _____ We only have to worry about "the two of us."

23. _____ The equity in my home is my retirement fund.

24. _____ If I save all of my money for retirement, I won't have fun living *now*.

Chapter Two

Your Retirement Planning Roadmap

Whether you're planning a revolution or simply making a commitment to take control of your retirement future, you need a fail-safe plan of action. To assure that you take advantage of your greatest retirement-planning tool—time—you must formulate a budget that allows you to save the little bit of money that will grow to be a lot of dough by the time you're ready to devote yourself to golf, grandchildren and/or grand tours.

A budget is your financial roadmap, showing you where you are *now* so you can effectively plan how to get where you *want* to be in the future.

A budget isn't a drain on your time; it's a time-saver.

A budget doesn't prevent you from having what you want; it helps you set spending and saving priorities so you can achieve the financial goals and objectives you desire most.

The importance of a budget

Too many consumers and their money are living so far apart that they are practically strangers. If you live only for today, you will pay for it tomorrow...and tomorrow...and tomorrow.

Complete the simple budget at the end of this chapter to get a firm handle on how much money you have coming in and going out each month. This chart will be the entire basis of all of your financial planning and absolutely essential to effective retirement planning. Proceeding without performing this step is worse than putting the cart before the horse. It's like trying to move the cart *without* a horse!

Remember: There will never be a better time, a cheaper time or a more convenient time than *right now* to start planning for your retirement.

As you go through the expense categories, use averages where necessary, particularly for items that will vary from month to month, such as heat, clothing, medical and dental bills,.

Even though every expense on this list will not be paid out monthly, the money should be available in checking or savings accounts so that juggling to pay bills does not deter you from your goal—putting away money for your golden years.

Pay yourself first

How will you pay these bills each month?

Well, if you're like most people, you'll write checks in the following order: mortgage or rent, utility bills, car payments, groceries, transportation and other living expenses, the monthly minimums on credit cards, time payments and miscellaneous expenses. Medical bills will usually go to the bottom of next month's pile—it takes doctors and dentists so long to send out dunning notices, doesn't it?

In order to save for retirement effectively, you should take a different approach: Make a payment to your savings account *first*. I recommend targeting 10% of your monthly net income, but if it must be less, at least make it *something*.

This notion of "paying yourself first" will force you to become more frugal in your spending habits—the bills left sitting there after you make that bank deposit still must be paid. Conversely, paying the bills first might encourage you to think of savings as something that can be safely put off...again.

That crazy little thing called savings

Your first goal with these payments to yourself is to build an emergency fund, a special account that can be used should (when) you have "one of those days"—you struggle to work after the transmission falls out of your car...just in time for your boss to hand you a pink slip.

Remember: This emergency fund should be at least 10% of your annual net income. Once that rainy day piggy bank is established, it's time to look at other savings goals. (Much more detailed advice on the overall budget process is available in my first book, **Get Rich Slow**, recently published in a brand-new second edition. And if you already know my advice on what to do with those savings, you'll want to get another of my **MONEY POWER** handbooks—**MONEY POWER Through Mutual Funds**).

You'd better stick like glue

Put your budget on the refrigerator so you see it daily and it reminds you about your commitment to your and your family's future.

Review this plan at least once a month. Make up your mind to stick to it. Reevaluate it from time to time. If temporary emergencies make it impossible to continue in the short-run, resume your new plan as quickly as possible.

Time to retire already?

How do you know how much you need to save to be able to afford retirement?

You have to develop a post-retirement budget, readjusting income and expenses for the day you bid goodby to your boss and head for the golf links.

As you start picturing your post-retirement lifestyle, perhaps you'll be able to knock a few lines off this budget, such as mortgage interest payments and college tuitions, and, most definitely, commuting expenses. On the other hand, you should probably increase the amount you budget for medical and dental expenses.

Examine your health insurance choices, keeping in mind that Medicare will not be available to you until age 65. Then review your death insurance policies and any retirement employer insurance benefits. Your major concern should be the escalating costs of living, not dying. (If you still need death insurance, purchase the cheaper term type. If you are not insurable, explore the group retirement options available through your employer. Don't purchase individual policies that overlook medical underwriting.)

When plugging anticipated Social Security payments into your budget, allow for 6% inflation on your living expenses and a 3% annual increase in Social Security payments. If longevity runs in your family, make plans for a longer lifespan than the national averages.

Preparing this second set of numbers is usually a very sobering experience. When some of my clients complete a post-retirement budget, they are amazed to see that their expenses will not decline that significantly, although their income will. The sooner you complete *both* budgets, the faster you can start saving to reach your goal.

You must start planning for your retirement well in advance of the time that you get your gold watch—two or three years, if possible. The checklist on p. 92 will help. Take the time to fill it out now...and make plans to complete it as soon as possible.

How much is enough?

The worksheets on pp. 34 and 35 will help you visualize how much you may need during your retirement period as well as how much you need to save per year to add to your retirement savings. They assume that your investments will grow at 8% per year and that inflation will continue at 5% on an annual basis.

On average, you should be able to produce a gross 10% rate of return per year. Like all averages, that expectation should be taken somewhat lightly—there will be years when you will not achieve your goal, others when you'll do even better.

All figures should be in today's dollars. Therefore, you should update this worksheet annually so it stays current with actual economic conditions.

MONTHLY CASH FLOW STATEMENT

Monthly Take-Home Pay: _____

Monthly Expenses: _____

Remaining Money (Take-Home Pay
Minus Expenses):   _____

Monthly Expense Detail

Savings and Investments: _____

> Include company pension plans, individual retirement plans (IRAs, Keoghs, etc.), establishing an emergency fund and general investment accounts.

Housing Costs

Monthly Mortgage Payment/Rent :   _____

Property Taxes (per month):   _____

Property Insurance(per month):   _____

Home Equity Loan Payments: _____

Consumer Debt

Dept. Store Accounts: _____

Credit Card Accounts: _____

Bank Loans: _____

Car Payment(s):   _____

Other Time Payments: _____

Other Monthly Expenses

*Auto Insurance: _____

*Car Maintenance: _____

*Child Support/Alimony: _____

*Clothing: _____

*Entertainment: _____

*Gasoline/Diesel: _____

*Groceries: _____

*Health Insurance: _____

*Household Items: _____

*Life Insurance: _____

*Medical/Dental: _____

*Miscellaneous: _____

*Organization Dues: _____

*Other Insurance: _____

*School Supplies: _____

*School Tuition: _____

*Student Loan or Tuition: _____

*Subscriptions: _____

*Telephone: _____

*Utilities: _____

*Vacation: _____

*Medicare Part B _____

*Medigap Insurance _____

*Long-term Care Insurance _____

Total: _____

If any of the above expenses are based on weekly out-go, multiply by **4.3** (weeks per month) to obtain accurate monthly figures (*not* by 4).

Personal Retirement Portfolio
Planning Worksheet

Short-term Retirement Objective:_____

Long-term Retirement Objective:_____

1. Cash and cash equivalents/short-term money (Checking and savings accounts, credit unions and rainy-day money)

Where Deposited	Objective	$ Value	Rate of Return
_____	_____	_____	_____
_____	_____	_____	_____
_____	_____	_____	_____
_____	_____	_____	_____
_____	_____	_____	_____
_____	_____	_____	_____
_____	_____	_____	_____
_____	_____	_____	_____

2. Securities/long-term money (bank CDs, annuities, mutual funds, stocks, bonds, etc.)

Investment or Security	Interest Rate	$ Value	Maturity Date
_____	_____	_____	_____
_____	_____	_____	_____

_____ _____ _____ _____

_____ _____ _____ _____

_____ _____ _____ _____

_____ _____ _____ _____

_____ _____ _____ _____

_____ _____ _____ _____

_____ _____ _____ _____

_____ _____ _____ _____

_____ _____ _____ _____

3. Regular Investment Programs

Name of Vehicle	Amount Invested	Frequency	Current Yield	Present Value

Retirement Worksheet

1. Annual gross income needed at retirement (90%-100% of current income in today's dollars, not adjusted for inflation) _____

2. Probable future Social Security benefits _____

3. Probable future company pension benefits _____
(If your company pension is integrated or combined with Social Security, complete only line 2 or 3, not both)

4. Add together line 2 and line 3 for total benefits _____

5. Annual retirement income needed from personal savings and investments (line 1 minus line 4) _____

6. Amount you must save before retirement (line 5 multiplied by Table A [page 36]) _____

7. Personal retirement savings already accumulated (this includes IRAs, annuities, 401ks not noted above, 403b or TSA plans, corporate savings plans, supplementary deferred compensation, company stock, or ESOPS, and miscellaneous investments earmarked for retirement needs.) _____

8. Projected future value of retirement savings at retirement time (line 7 multiplied by Table B [page 37]) _____

9. Amount of retirement capital still needed (line 6 minus line 8) _____

10. Annual savings needed to reach your goal (line 9 multiplied by Table C [page 37]) _____

11. Annual savings needed (line 10 minus annual employer contributions to retirement funds) _____

Sample Retirement Worksheet

1. Annual gross income needed at retirement (90%-100% of current income in today's dollars, not adjusted for inflation) $40,000

2. Probable future Social Security benefits $12,000

3. Probable future company pension benefits (If your company pension is integrated or combined with Social Security, complete only line 2 or 3, not both.) $8,000

4. Add together line 2 and line 3 for total benefits $20,000

5. Annual retirement income needed from personal savings and investments (line 1 minus line 4) $20,000

6. Amount you must save before retirement (line 5 multiplied by Table A [next page]) $384,000

7. Personal retirement savings already accumulated $200,000

8. Projected future value of retirement savings at retirement time (line 7 multiplied by Table B [page 37]) $258,000

9. Amount of retirement capital still needed (line 6 minus line 8) $126,000

10. Annual savings needed to reach your goal (line 9 multiplied by Table C [page 37]) $12,474

11. Annual savings needed (line 10 minus annual employer contributions to retirement funds) $7,474

Projected Monthly Social Security Benefits

(Top line is worker's current annual salary)

Worker's Current Age	$30,000	$40,000	$50,000	$55,000+
45 Worker	1,159	1,302	1,436	1,491
45 w/spouse	1,738	1,953	2,154	2,236
55 Worker	1,052	1,150	1,231	1,258
55 w/spouse	1,578	1,725	1,846	1,887
65 Worker	977	1,038	1,081	1,088
65 w/spouse	1,465	1,557	1,621	1,632

These figures are for a worker who has enjoyed steady lifetime earnings and is retiring in 1992. Use this table only to "guessti-mate" what you may be eligible for at your retirement age. This is insufficient as a retirement plan unless there is additional income to supplement these payments. Source: Social Security Administration, 1992

Table A

Age at Retirement	Retirement Factor A
55	23.3
56	22.9
57	22.6
58	22.2
59	21.8
60	21.4
61	21.0
62	20.5
63	20.1
64	19.6
65	19.2
66	18.7
67	18.2

Table B

Years to Retirement	Retirement Factor B
5	1.15
7	1.22
9	1.29
11	1.36
13	1.44
15	1.53
20	1.76
25	2.02
30	2.33

Table C

Years to Retirement	Retirement Factor C
5	0.188
7	0.131
9	0.099
11	0.079
13	0.065
15	0.054
20	0.038
25	0.028
30	0.022

The factors used in these worksheets assume a hypothetical 8% before-tax return and a 5% inflation rate. They are only to be used as a general guideline. Always consult your tax advisor before making major financial decisions.

Chapter Three

Social *In*security: What's It Worth To You?

Social Security is based on the principle that part of the responsibility for the loss of an individual's income due to retirement, disability, death or medical needs should be born by society as a whole.

Supported through employee/employer payroll taxes, it is a pay-as-you-go program, with current workers paying benefits to those now receiving monthly payments. Controversies over how well the program is funded should caution future retirees not to depend on this or any social program for their total retirement financial comfort.

Retirement benefits are figured on covered work credits and are related to career employment earnings. There is a weighted formula applied for each case. Participation during the working phase of most employees' lives is compulsory.

Benefits are not necessarily based on the amount the individual has contributed to the system in the past. The current benefits are not meant to totally replace a worker's wages and should be supplemented through other sources of retirement income.

Applying for benefits

Contact the Social Security Administration three months before you plan to sign up (either at age 62, 65 or before age 70). If you have not applied for Social Security benefits by age 65, be sure you *do* apply for Medicare (which is automatically available at age 65 whether you continue to work or not).

When you apply, Social Security will send you appropriate application forms and related materials. If family members are eligible, they should also apply.

You will need the following information to apply:

1. Your Social Security number;

2. Proof of your age;

3. Proof of marriage (if applying for widow or widower's benefits);

4. Proof of divorce (if applying as a divorced widow or widower);

5. Proof of a worker's death (if this qualified you for benefits);

6. Children's birth certificates and Social Security numbers (if they are to receive any payment);

7. Proof of support (if applying as a dependent parent or grandchild of a deceased worker).

If you bring records of your checking or savings account, Social Security can arrange to have your benefits deposited directly into the account. This may be a safer method of payment than receiving your monthly check in the mail. You can also opt to have your payment for Medicare Part B automatically deducted from your monthly Social Security check.

A one-time lump sum benefit of $255 is paid at the death of a covered retiree. This must be applied for separately, accompanied by a certified death certificate.

Washington's "disincentive" plan

If you were born before 1938, your normal retirement age for full Social Security benefits (if you qualify) is your 65th birthday. For birthdates from 1938 on, the age for collecting a full monthly benefit payment begins to roll backward. Today's younger worker won't qualify for full retirement benefits until age 67.

When you reach that magic age, you can receive monthly payments for the remainder of your life if you have earned enough credits. Since we all know that Social Security is only a supplement and not meant—even jokingly—to represent a decent retirement income, your first instinct should be to continue working right past retirement age to add to the nominal monthly payment.

Unfortunately, this makes far too much sense for our elected legislators, who pay farmers not to plant food, while children, families and some elderly citizens slowly starve. Even farmers think that concept makes little sense. But given that program, we might as well also pay retirees to sit home and develop arthritis and clogged arteries instead of encouraging them to keep working so they can support themselves in a more dignified manner.

How do we demotivate retirees? Social Security benefits may be reduced until age 70 for those who earn too much (from Washington's standpoint) income per year. This requirement applies to both retirees and disabled persons.

While under age 65, for every two dollars you earn above the annual exempted amount, one dollar will be *deducted* from your monthly Social Security benefits. If you are between 65 and 70, the reduction is one dollar in benefits for every three dollars in earnings above the exempted amount.

What is the exempted amount? It changes according to inflation on an annual basis. Contact your Social Security office for the current earned income ceiling.

What wages are counted as earned income for purposes of reducing your benefits? Salary, bonuses, commissions, fees, vacation pay or pay in lieu of vacation time, cash tips of $20 or more per month, severance pay and certain non-cash compensation such as meals or living accommodations.

Income *not* counted for reduction purposes includes investment income, interest, Social Security or Veteran's benefits, insurance or company pension annuities, capital gains, gifts, inheritances, rental income (unless you sell real estate as a business or participate in the management of farm products), royalties, trust fund income, some sick pay, moving expenses, travel expenses and jury duty pay. Consult your tax advisor for specific details.

You must file an annual report in addition to your regular tax return. You may also need to repay some benefits if you have underestimated your earnings. A penalty may be assessed if you do not file a timely or correct report.

Though you must file an annual report when you become 70, your earnings won't affect your monthly benefits. Whoopee!

There are prorated rules for those retiring during the year based on which month they apply for Social Security benefits. Contact their offices to make the optimum decision.

In addition to a possible reduction in benefits, you may be taxed on up to half of your Social Security payment if your total income exceeds $25,000 per year for singles and $32,000 for married couples filing jointly. The tax due is on the lesser of 1/2 of your Social Security benefits or 1/2 of the amount of your adjusted gross income exceeding the figures mentioned above.

After age 70, if you can stay alive on below-poverty level earnings so your Social Security payments won't be reduced, you can begin to work full-time with no threat of reduced monthly payments.

Earning less income so your retirement benefits will not be reduced or taxed may be Congress' idea of expedient tax planning. But if you create too little income during the first stage of retirement, you may run out of savings before your final demise. We all know there are only two things we can count on—death and taxes. Be careful not to accelerate the former by applying too much of the latter.

Spousal rights

A divorced spouse may have the same right as a married spouse to Social Security benefits. Even if the insured worker has remarried, the divorced spouse should investigate this option. However, if the divorced spouse remarries, he or she may lose such rights to benefits of the insured worker's record. Ordinarily, a divorced spouse loses Social Security rights when he or she remarries. But benefits may continue without any reduction for a widow or widower who remarries after age 60, or for a disabled widow or widower who remarries after age 50.

When a worker starts collecting retirement or disability payments, the divorced spouse may receive benefits if:

- He or she is age 62 or older;
- He or she does not qualify for benefits that equal or exceed 1/2 of the worker's full amount; and
- He or she was married to the worker for at least 10 years.

The benefits of the divorced spouse do not negatively affect any benefits the worker or the worker's current spouse may be receiving.

Even if the worker is not actually receiving benefits, the divorced spouse can get retirement payments at age 62 if the worker is eligible for benefits and they have been divorced for at least two years.

Chapter Four

Medical Care And Medicare: What You Should Know

Unfortunately, the older we get, the sicker we get. For many retirees, health care is the biggest item in their budgets, often becoming an expense that bankrupts them and steals their dreams for rewarding themselves after decades of hard work.

This chapter will discuss what you can do to keep doctors, prescriptions and hosptials from taking all of your savings.

Everyone's entitlement program

Parts A and B of Medicare are Uncle Sam's presents to you on your 65th birthday. Part A pays for hospitalization, post-hospital skilled nursing facility care, home health care, hospice care and blood transfusions. Part B pays for medical expenses, home health care, outpatient hospital treatments and trans-fusions.

Part A has no premium. It is part of the social insurance health program, funded through payroll taxes, to which Americans are entitled based on age, not need. Part B carries a small premium which increases yearly but is, nevertheless, a pittance compared with the benefits it provides.

Medicare provides beneficiaries protection against financial turmoil that can be brought about by the stratospheric costs of health care. It has, like all other government programs, a long list of rules that I will do my best to clarify in this chapter.

For those still working

Sometimes Medicare kicks in only after other insurance plans pay their share. For instance, the law requires larger employers to offer the same health benefits to workers and spouses age 65 or older that they provide to younger workers. If you continue working after age 65, or if you are 65 or older and married to a worker, you have the option to reject the employer's health plan and pick up Medicare as your primary health carrier.

If you reject the employer's general health plan, however, the employer is not allowed to offer you Medicare supplemental or Medigap health coverage.

If you are less than 65 and eligible for Medicare due to disability (other than kidney failure), Medicare will be your secondary health carrier if you choose your employer's health plan or a family member's employer health plan as your first choice.

When you have an employer health plan and Medicare is a secondary carrier, you can wait to enroll in Medicare medical insurance. This enrollment period begins either within the month you stop working or the month the employer plan ends (for any reason), whichever comes first. You will not have to pay the 10% annual premium surcharge for late enrollment.

There's more confusion here

If you are an accident victim, Medicare is the secondary carrier of your health insurance benefits after your auto medical insurance or that of the other driver, your state no-fault insurance program or someone's liability insurance coverage.

For those on permanent kidney failure treatment, Medicare is the secondary carrier for the first 12 months. After that, Medicare becomes their primary carrier.

If the primary insurer's payments for medical expenses are considered full payment, Medicare has no additional liability to pay secondary benefits to supplement those primary payments.

Whenever confused about who is supposed to pay (and who wouldn't be, given that the preceding is my English *translation* of the less understandable Government gobbledegook?), contact your Medicare office for another try at translation.

Medicare supplements

If you think the Medicare rules are complex, try ferreting through the fine print—the paragraphs on risks, time limit on defenses, exclusions, and limitations—while searching for a Medigap insurance policy that you can be sure will pay when you need supplemental health coverage.

Medicare, Medigap and Medicaid are made even more complicated by the insurance industry's marketing of supplemental health coverage.

Comparison shopping is supposed to become easier now that there are ten standard categories insurance companies legally must adhere to. But abuse is still rampant in this type of health insurance.

To help insure that you don't get ripped off, avoid buying any kind of insurance from a door-to-door salesperson or on the advice of friends and neighbors. They can't read their contracts any better than you can.

Start your research at the library, using consumer magazines that rate various insurance companies. Don't depend on endorsements from any organization, even those that focus on assistance to the elderly. Read through the clauses and sections that outline the limitations and exclusions of the product, and avoid those who can insure you too quickly. They might sign you up without any medical underwriting, then decide whether to pay after you turn in a claim.

Never buy on the first sales presentation, especially in your home. You are not purchasing a vacuum cleaner—this is your catastrophic health care backup. Listen to several agents' sales pitches and ask them to compare other companies' policies to theirs. Don't compare prices. Compare benefits and value.

Insurance jargon takes on a life of its own. Terms can be very deceptive. So be careful about "interpreting" the insurance language—your translation might be totally different than what the insurance company is actually promising (or not promising).

Long-term care insurance

My cautions are the same to those purchasing nursing home and custodial care insurance. I even hesitate recommending that someone in their 50s purchase such insurance at all today. The health care and nursing home managed-care environment will be so different in 10 or 15 years that more folks will be cared for in their own homes.

Many of today's policies offer less generous benefits for home health care. Policies in the future will undoubtedly encourage the use of lower-cost health care solutions.

Some areas to look for when comparing long-term insurance contracts are:

1. No prior hospitalization requirements;
2. Substantial coverages for intermediate or custodial care, no matter what facilities are used;

3. Reasonable time limitations on pre-existing health conditions;

4. A higher daily benefit and longer waiting period before benefits begin. This reduces the premium but keeps the most important benefit intact;

5. Language stating that the policy is ***non-cancellable, guaranteed renewable, at a guaranteed premium.*** Even in policies with such language, watch for subsequent clauses that describe (believe it or not) how the company can "non-renew" the policy;

6. Unlimited benefits for unlimited periods of time (or *at least* three years) in a nursing home residence. The less time, the less valuable the insurance.

For any type of health insurance, do *not* purchase *any*thing until you:

1. Consider more than one policy;

2. Obtain and read a specimen policy from each agent whose company you are considering;

3. Research how a company is rated by *several* rating agencies;

4. Compare policy contract language with that in other insurance contracts;

5. Ask agents to compare their products against others; in the old days, this was called "competition." Interesting concept.

Beyond smiles and prices

You don't care how pretty or handsome the agent looks, how nicely they may be dressed, or how friendly they are while they are searching for your checkbook. You must play the role of "Grambo," on the lookout for suspicious-sounding promises when they veer from the written contract language.

In the passion of a sale, an agent may promise anything. Never purchase out of greed or fear. All policies are not created equal. Don't bend to fear tactics that you may not be insurable by anyone else. If other companies aren't interested in your business, why is the one this agent is pitching?

There may be little relationship between higher premiums and better quality, but cheap premiums can mean inferior benefits. Be careful when a policy seems *too* affordable. There are no "sales" in the uncertain and risky health arena.

All insurance companies are in business to make a profit. Ignore company advertising. Marketing tells you absolutely nothing about the real value of any insurance contract or the company.

There are additional pitfalls. Read over the medical section and fully answer every question. Don't leave any blanks or trust the agent to fill them in after he or she gets back to the office.

If an agent refuses to write down your response to a medical question, insist that it is marked anyway. A dishonest agent could omit serious medical information that might cause benefits to be later denied.

When you sign an insurance application, you are taking full responsibility for the veracity of all your answers, whether you or the insurance agent filled out the application.

Request a specimen policy before you purchase a real contract. No one would purchase a car without first kicking the tires, and no one should purchase something as important as health care without first seeing the merchandise.

After you receive your insurance policy, read it thoroughly. You have a "free-look" provision that allows you to return it for a full refund within a certain period of time. If you do not receive your written contract within a reasonable time, call the company directly to see what has happened and to be sure the agent isn't holding it past the time when you could reject it without charge.

If you return your policy, the agent will lose his or her commission. This is not an incentive for him or her to cooperate in your cancellation! So you must be persistent and call the insurance company directly for instructions on how to proceed if you decide to cancel.

The health care and long-term-care environments are dynamic areas. Good financial consumers shop for insurance in the same manner they shop for groceries: by comparing benefits and prices and by investigating for themselves.

Medicaid programs

Medicaid is a last resort health subsidy funded by a combination of state and federal programs. It is designed for the financially impoverished. Its regulations are restrictive—to qualify, applicants must have few financial reserves or other forms of property.

How do people with significant assets still manage to qualify for Medicaid? A common strategy is to purchase a long-term-care nursing home policy that will self-pay from the time they transfer their assets out of their name to the date they qualify for their state Medicaid program.

As more qualified entrants fill Medicaid rolls, the rules will likely be changed and exclude those who *could* pay but, through such strategies, manage to qualify for a program designed primarily for the indigent.

Costs aren't coming down

Future medical care costs will absorb the largest portion of your retirement savings. Employer programs and social insurance formats will change: You may be responsible for a larger share of your own health care costs.

When shopping today for health care insurance, carefully evaluate the choice between a health maintenance organization (HMO) plan (a cheaper solution) and a more traditional health care plan that demands a larger deductible and a bigger co-payment by you, but allows you to use the physicians of your choice. As managed cost-effective health care struggles for fiscal soundness, HMOs' lower cost will look more attractive; current systems are priced higher to limit their access by the general populace.

Weigh these alternatives carefully before you choose— eventually you may not be able to reverse your decision.

Chapter Five

Taming Your Post-Retirement Tax Bite

Once you "retire" from earning a paycheck, you don't, unfortunately, "retire" from paying taxes.

However, the *way* you pay those taxes will change. For one thing, you'll be on your own, responsible for making quarterly payments to Uncle Sam—no more job, no more withholding. In addition, you'll be paying different types of taxes on such things as supplemental pensions, insurance annuities, and interest or dividends, all of which have their own tax consequences.

Some tax traps

You'll have to worry about several new tax traps as you make the adjustment from full-time employee to comptroller of the 18th hole:

(1) *Underestimating your quarterly tax liability.* To avoid this (and a penalty for underpayment of current taxes), ask your accountant or a competent tax preparer to forecast your tax payments throughout the year.

(2) *Incorrectly calculating taxes on investments such as mutual funds.* The annual 1099 form from your mutual fund company will show only the fund's taxable distributions during the year. If you sell any of your shares, there might be an additional capital gains tax due on the profit you earned above your original purchase price.

Some mutual funds send a statement detailing all selling activity and the cost basis (original cost) of the shares you sold. Your accountant will want this to determine your tax consequences. (Another of my books in this series—**MONEY POWER Through Mutual Funds**—teaches strategies to neutralize taxes on the sale of mutual funds.)

(3) *Treating a mutual fund exchange as a nontaxable event.* Any time you exchange from one mutual fund to another (even one in the same fund family) outside of an IRA or other pension program, there is a tax consequence. Any gain or profit on the price of the shares sold (including those that have been reinvested) will be taxed along with other income your fund distributed.

Fund-hopping for short-term profits or to time the markets will hurt you, because each time you change funds, Uncle Sam shares part of your booty.

(4) *Ignoring the alternative minimum tax because you are not rich.* The alternative

minimum tax (AMT) formula can trigger a tax on middle-income retirees without their knowledge. Many retired investors purchase tax-favored investments believing it is simply smarter investing. But most tax-free income is added back into your income when determining whether you must pay this special tax.

(5) *Missing the opportunity to cash out on your home.* After age 55, you have a one-time opportunity to eliminate up to $125,000 of deferred profits built up over the years as you bought and sold your homes. If you eventually sell and purchase a smaller home or just decide to rent, you can write-off as much as $125,000 of the profits from this final sale.

You must have lived in the residence for three out of the last five years and declare it as your primary residence for this tax break to apply. Neither spouse can have taken this exclusion before, and, again, you must be age 55 or older.

(6) *Taking a deduction for a non-deductible IRA.* If you are eligible for or actively involved in a company pension plan and earn more than a certain income, part or all of your annual IRA contribution might be ineligible for an immediate tax deduction. File a Form 8606 with your Form 1040 tax return to record how much of your IRA is non-deductible. That will assure it will not be taxed again when you eventually start drawing from your IRA account after retirement.

(7) *Stopping your annual IRA contribution after retirement age.* As long as you continue to earn income, you are eligible to continue contributing to an IRA account (until age 70). IRA money is special investment capital because it is

tax-deferred until withdrawn. You will need every advantage to keep your dollars working hard for you until they are finally spent.

(8) ***Writing checks against mutual fund accounts.*** Each time you write a check against your mutual fund, you are actually selling shares of your account. These transactions might trigger a capital gains tax on those shares sold if their price has increased from when you bought them. Ask your tax advisor to calculate the consequences.

(9) ***Mistaking a line of credit for a tax-deductible home equity loan.*** Not all loans collateralized by your home are authentic second mortgages deductible from your taxes. Request your loan officer to define clearly what type of money you are borrowing. Then check with your tax advisor to find out if it is deductible.

It generally makes little sense to borrow a dollar just because you can deduct 28¢ of it from your taxes. You should carefully consider the need to borrow at all when you reach retirement age. You are putting your house on the block at a time when your income will be fixed or even substantially in decline.

(10) ***Deducting points from a refinancing loan all at once.*** Refinancing points must be written off over the life of the new loan. Only loan-origination fees incurred when purchasing or remodeling your home may be immediately deducted. Be sure you understand the difference.

(11) ***Waiting to start IRA distributions until the year after you turn 70 1/2.*** If you do, you must withdraw *two* distributions in that year—one for the prior year, one for the current calendar year.

This could increase your tax liability in that year and may result in the taxation of Social Security payments. Program your income to plan the optimum method of distribution for your financial circumstances.

(12) *Withdrawing IRA funds, pensions, insurance annuities or other retirement accounts before age 59 1/2.* Generally, if you take your money before age 59 1/2, you will incur an additional 10% penalty along with the taxes due on all your before-tax contributions and the earnings on them.

After age 59 1/2, the 10% penalty disappears, and you are liable only for taxes due on the pre-tax money and earnings you withdraw.

There are exceptions to these general rules, so consult your tax advisor. Resist the temptation to withdraw funds earmarked for retirement. The tax consequences are so severe that you will wind up with less than you thought *and* have destroyed seed dollars that could have compounded over time to create the miracles you need throughout your retirement years.

(13) *Neglecting to fill out a tax Form 8606 for non-deductible IRA contributions.* If some part of your post-1986 IRA funds are non-deductible, they will be taxed *before* you invest them. If you do not keep adequate records of which funds have already been taxed, they might be taxed *again* when you withdraw them many years later. Paying taxes once is quite enough!

(14) *Forgetting some IRA funds when calculating mandatory IRA distributions after age 70 1/2.* You must add the total value of *all* IRA money before determining how much to with-

draw on an annual basis. This number is based on the total value of all IRA money as of December 31st of the previous calendar year.

(15) ***Refusing to calculate other IRA withdrawal options.*** There are three basic methods for determining how much you must withdraw annually from your IRA accounts:

First, you may use the current tables to calculate your life expectancy and continue with the same formula for the remainder of your life.

Second, you may choose to reevaluate or recalculate your life expectancy using new IRA annuity tables each year. This method might allow you to withdraw less money at a time.

Finally, you may combine your calculated life expectancy with that of your IRA beneficiary (within certain limits) to determine how much money you must withdraw. A younger beneficiary or a female spouse has a longer life expectancy. That will reduce the amount you must withdraw.

Important caveat: Once you start using one method, you must continue in that manner.

These formulas can be complex, and mistakes carry heavy penalties. Get a professional to do these calculations for you unless you are determined to shoulder the task yourself. If you do, at least go over your calculations with an IRS employee before you turn in your tax form.

(16) ***Mistaking a hobby for a small business.*** Many retirees open small businesses for leisure and extra income. You must keep track of all receipts, sales and business expenses. Quarterly taxes might need to be filed, payroll taxes might be due.

To prove your business purpose, you must make a profit in three out of five years or provide records that prove you are trying to stay in the black.

Request the IRS publications for small businesses, business use of a vehicle and small business taxation. You might also need a state vendor's license and advice regarding state sales tax procedures.

(17) *Earning enough income to reduce your Social Security payments.* The sad commentary on our times is that your government will pay folks not to work. From age 62 to age 65, your Social Security will be reduced *one* dollar for every *two* dollars to which you are entitled if you earn more than a specific amount (which changes each year). From age 65 to age 70, the penalty is less severe: One dollar less for every *three* dollars you would otherwise receive.

Once you turn 70, you are free to earn all the income you can produce. But hardening of the arteries and your arthritis from sitting around so much might limit your ability to run for the 7:30 am bus so you can work a 40-hour week right up to the day of your funeral.

(18) *Triggering taxes on your Social Security payments by earning too much total income.* Currently, Social Security payments of singles who make more than $25,000 in both earned and unearned income are taxed. Married couples can earn $32,000 together before their Social Security payments are taxed.

If you are worried that you might outlive your savings, tax planning through slow starvation is ridiculous. Decide whether you can afford to create less income or whether you will be better off working while you can, even though you might receive fewer government dollars or have them taxed because of these senseless laws.

(19) ***Not keeping comprehensive records of home improvement over the years.*** When you sell your home, your original cost is increased by the amount you spent on home improvements, along with all the costs of selling your house. Your profit—that amount on which you must pay taxes—is derived by subtracting this cost basis from the amount you received from the buyer. Needless to say, the more expenses you are able to add, the greater your cost basis, the less your profit and the less taxes you must pay. So keep excellent records of everything that may increase that basis. (I am presuming you have to worry about taxes on profits because you cannot take the $125,000 exclusion discussed earlier in this chapter.)

(20) ***Believing everything you read or hear about avoiding taxes.*** So much misinformation exists that retirees can make serious mistakes by considering tax planning a first priority. There are more important criteria to consider than avoiding taxes, like choosing better quality investments and taking less risk on your precious investment dollars.

Your main objective should be creating *income*, not tax losses.

When you need tax help

Tax simplification has made things more and more complicated. If members of Congress filled out their own tax returns, things would become easier for all of us in a hurry. But they can afford to pay someone else to sweat over the sometimes impossible rules.

Think twice before performing your own operation if you have one or more of the following items:

1. *Rental property.* You must calculate depreciation whether you want to or not, and the steps can be mind boggling, with a maze of old and new rules intertwined together.

2. *Passive losses or gains* (including limited partnership K-1 forms). Many of you would like to forget the pain involved in past partnership experiences. But they keep coming, and you must keep paying to file them. Passive activities are business interests in which you do not play an active role. The rules are complicated and should not be attempted by most taxpayers.

3. *IRA mandatory distributions.* If you tackle the challenge, at least have the forms reviewed by the IRS or a tax advisor. You must use the proper life expectancy tables and estimate your correct age as of this calendar year. Mistakes can be severely penalized—a 50% penalty for withdrawing too little from your IRA funds.

4. *Alternative minimum tax.* It was designed to create a level playing field between those who invested in tax-advantaged investments and the rest of us who invested in three college tuitions, two sets of braces, and three replacements of Monopoly because when *our* kids were growing up, there was little money for any other type of entertainment.

   If you thrive on passive loss rules and tax preference items, go for it. Otherwise, pay someone else to burn the midnight oil while you sleep soundly.

5. ***Installment sales.*** When you spread out a buyer's payment over a number of years, you encounter some complicated tax rules. Installment sales can be tricky. Tax pros know how to communicate with the IRS more clearly than you probably do.

With today's computer technology, tax filing is easier than ever. Weigh the savings of do-it-yourself filing with the frustrations and possible consequences your amateur status may engender.

In the near future, I expect to see the ultimate in tax simplification: A two-line form that merely asks, "How much did you make last year?" then tells you where to send it.

Chapter Six

Better Solutions For Your Pension Than Insurance

Just when you thought it was safe to go back into the financial waters, those friendly and helpful insurance agents you've been avoiding for most of your adult life will approach you with a list of new and improved suggestions for retirement income and investing. Beware! Insurance solutions for retirement planning are generally ineffective, often deceptively sold, and supply none of their supposed benefits in a cost-effective manner.

Commissions 'r' us

Salespeople, hot on the trail of large commission checks, will promise to resurrect you from low-yielding, unsafe and taxable investments when you really *should* be investing in vehicles like bank CDs and mutual funds.

In the insurance world, whole life or savings insurance policies pay the largest commissions, followed closely by fixed and variable annuities. The last thing an insurance agent who may himself be close to retirement wants you to do is find cheaper term insurance and invest your savings in a real mutual fund.

This chapter explores some popular insurance solutions and the reasons you should steer clear of them.

The IRA alternative

You might be told that smart investors are now looking for alternative investments for their former (now non-deductible) IRA dollars. Insurance company representatives will tell you that now you can have your very own private pension plan with tax-favored status.

Here are some benefits you may be shown: tax-deferred earnings; high current interest rates; no income limitations on eligibility; flexible deposits that can exceed $2,000 per year; no penalty for distribution before age 59 1/2; a guaranteed income that you cannot outlive; no reduction in Social Security payments; an income tax-free death benefit; and finally, tax-free income through loans. All this generally comes with a guarantee of principal.

The sizzle sounds so attractive that some consumers never realize the steak they have purchased is a whole life insurance policy, the same vehicle that caused their parents to subsist near the poverty level after retirement.

Attractive ledger sheets are meaningless. An agent could put anything down on paper, depending on how gullible he or she thought the customer might be. Proposed interest rates only apply to the meager amounts left *after* the insurance company (and its agent) take out their share of your premium. In other words, you get X% of what's left *after* commissions, loads, mortality charges, etc.

The tax-deferred nature of an insurance policy is rather impotent considering the *real* (i.e., low) rate of return on your investment. When you want your money, you must borrow it from yourself or withdraw it taxably; and every dollar you take is subtracted from your death benefit.

It's a clever industry that can teach consumers to borrow their own money, pay a fortune in premiums at an older age for the insurance protection inside, then hand them a contract so complicated that it would take a Philadelphia lawyer to translate it into plain English.

If you need death insurance at retirement time, purchase a cheaper term policy. Take the remainder of your premium dollars and invest in some high quality diversified mutual funds instead of in your local insurance agent's retirement home in Boca Raton or Honolulu.

To max or not to max: That is the pension

As retirement nears, you will examine the pension options available in your employee retirement package. You may have the following choices:

1. A lump sum distribution you can roll over into an IRA and manage yourself to keep the funds tax-deferred;

2. A monthly pension check for the remainder of your life only;

3. A smaller (usually 10% less) monthly pension payment for you and a spouse's life—a joint and survivor annuity.

You may wrestle with this decision, but any self-respecting insurance agent worth his vested retirement pension already knows which option is right for you. He or she will recommend you take the larger monthly pension payment for your life only and purchase a whole life or universal life insurance policy with some of the extra monthly cash you have snatched back from your company.

They will show you how easily you can afford this option with serious-looking ledger sheets, and all for a mere fraction of the extra money they have found for you.

Since you were probably severely underinsured during your most critical earning years—while your family was growing up—this solution might ease your sense of guilt. After all, it's not your money you'll be spending—it's your employer's.

This technique is called pension maximization and is abused by career insurance agents calling themselves estate and retirement planners. You need every penny for yourself so when the morning toast costs $3.50 a loaf, you will be able to afford lunch and dinner too.

Decline your agent's offer and search for some cheap term insurance, the real premium for which will be lower than the reduction of the joint and survivor pension option. If you can fund a death benefit large enough to pay your spouse similar survivor payments for the remainder of his or her life (according to the life expectancy tables), you will have found a winning strategy. Otherwise, choose the lump sum option or the survivorship benefit.

Look before you buy

Due to the insurance industry's current financial midlife crisis, buying any type of insurance is a leap of faith. So, even before buying term insurance, research a company as carefully as if you were marrying it. Your piece of mind and a vital death benefit depends on your choice.

If your insurance contract later becomes more useful as bathroom wallpaper and you are unhealthy or, worse yet, deceased, your insurance agent will not invite your spouse to live at his home.

Compare *all* the rating services at your local library. A.M. Best's rating is not enough. Check out Standard and Poor's,

Moody's, Duff and Phelps, and even Martin Weiss of Florida. An agent who tries to dissuade you from investigating may be afraid their ratings won't reinforce their fervent sales presentation. You want an insurance company that will be in business many years from now.

Don't purchase on price alone. Find the most solvent companies first. Then look for the best consumer value. Keep in mind that there is no life insurance—only death insurance. It just sells better by its more palatable name.

The better options

Your research on insurance products will confirm what I have told you: Your agent's atttractive ledger sheets are nothing more than marketing hype. Pass up your agent's advice and memorize *this* advice instead: The greater the lump sum offered by your company retirement plan, the more prudent it is to transfer it as an IRA rollover. You can work your own money as well as any stranger would, watch it more closely, perhaps even create higher returns.

If you choose one of the annuity payment options, what will happen if your company flies south with the geese in a few years? Who will guarantee the necessary monthly checks then?

If you choose either the lump sum option or the single life annuity payment, you must butter up your spouse because his or her written approval is necessary. Both choices leave him or her out of any future payments should you die first.

Time is the greatest risk factor of all. By opting for monthly payments of any kind for the rest of your life, you are betting your financial well being that your company will stay in business. A gamble in today's corporate and economic environment.

Fixed insurance annuities

These fears convince many consumers to turn to insurance annuities. They sound attractive because they offer higher returns, safety of principal and tax deferral. But unless you have been lost in the bush for the past two years, you have surely read that some insurance companies are closing their doors on their customers, locking up policy-holder money while state agencies and the corporations themselves argue over ways to keep the company in business.

In the meantime, their policy holders are not sleeping as well as they once did.

The insurance industry currently suffers from the same greed and mismanagement syndrome that hit S&Ls in the 1980s. Many companies are suffering from declining market values of junk bonds, too many hurricanes and tornados, and commercial real estate in the wrong locations.

When you invest in a fixed annuity, you transfer your dollars into the general checking account of the insurance company, which spends some of it on commissions and expenses and then invests the rest. In return, you own a piece of paper, a lifetime promise—good for the company's lifetime, not necessarily yours.

I would rather diversify my investment capital, be able to track my money daily and choose what types of investments I want.

I also want a larger share of the profits and accessibility to my funds at all times without surrender charges or early withdrawal penalties. After all, it *is* my money.

Insurance annuities (whether fixed or variable) are one of the least flexible investments you can purchase. You have limited information about how your assets are managed. The insurance agent gets a fat commission and you get the risk if the company fails in the future. Sound fair to you?

Variable annuities are advertised as mutual funds with a tax-deferred insurance wrapper. In truth, they are expensive, fee-laden, mutual fund look-alikes. Some tout popular mutual fund house names to attract investors. But names mean little if a nobody is managing your variable account, while extracting fees and expenses on an annual basis.

Administration expenses and annual mortality charges weigh these segregated accounts down. A mutual fund investor would never put up with such large annual fees for doing so little.

Purchase a better investment vehicle—a *real* mutual fund—and, if necessary, pay your tax bill. Variable annuities are no bargain when two sets of fees and expenses are extracted before you earn your share of the profits.

They are touted as safer than fixed-insurance annuities because they are separated from the general assets of the company. Call me an iconoclast, but I'm simply not convinced that if push came to shove, a company in financial stress couldn't find *some* loophole through which to siphon this supposedly "untouchable" money.

Chapter Seven

Estate Planning Made Easier

While it's certainly true that you can't take it with you, you can determine who gets it through good estate planning.

This is an area made complicated by federal legislation, as well as laws that vary from state to state. This chapter will provide general guidelines on putting together an estate plan that will most effectively carry out your wishes for who winds up with your hard-earned assets.

If you're thinking that estate planning is not necessary because you're not a millionaire, think again. An effective estate plan can reduce or altogether eliminate many of the probate and other problems faced by countless heirs to middle-class fortunes.

You need an estate plan if you:

1. Are married;
2. Have children;

3. Have been divorced;

4. Are widowed;

5. Have remarried;

6. Own tangible or financial property;

7. Owe debts and have financial obligations;

8. Own liquid assets in banks, credit unions, etc.;

9. Have a company pension;

10. Own group employer or individual death (life) insurance;

11. Own real estate or personal assets in another (ancillary) state;

12. Have a disabled spouse or other family member;

13. Are financially responsible for someone else;

14. Have had recent health problems;

15. Have had significant changes in your state's estate laws;

16. Intend to disinherit any of your relatives;

Even consumers with simple estates should have a *will* and a *durable power of attorney* (which allows someone you trust to manage your financial affairs in case of temporary or permanent disability).

In many states, it is also advisable to create a living or medical will. This living will might be a combination of medical instructions and a health care power of attorney so a family member can make health or medical decisions for you if you cannot. Consult your local or county bar association for guidelines regarding documents appropriate in your area.

Other simple estate-planning tools

Will substitutes are simple ways to pass your assets on to your heirs outside of probate and with little or no expense. The list includes, but is not limited, to the following:

1. Real estate survivorship deeds between spouses or grown children and their parents;

2. Bank savings, CDs, credit union, checking or money market accounts in joint names;

3. Bank accounts or savings made payable at your death to one or more beneficiaries;

4. IRA, SEP, KEOGH, TSA, 401k, and other pension beneficiary clauses;

5. Mutual funds or other securities in joint ownership (joint tenants with rights of survivorship);

6. Savings bonds in co-ownership or survivorship titles;

7. Auto titles in joint names;

8. Survivor benefit options on insurance or pension annuities.

Insurance policies should contain both a primary (first) and a contingent (secondary) *adult* beneficiary—no insurance company is going to send a $100,000 check to a three-year-old. Without an alternate plan, insurance proceeds will be directed into the will and, therefore, go through probate before being assigned as you directed.

You can name an adult for the benefit of your minor children in the policy and provide a contingent (just-in-case) trust and trustee inside your will for managing your assets in the event of a common disaster (the coincidental loss of both parents).

IRA accounts, pension plan proceeds, group death employer insurance at work, insurance annuities, and other retirement or employee benefits should also list primary and secondary beneficiaries.

Where there's a will, there's usually a way

However, no matter how little you own, dying *intestate* (without a will) creates difficulties for those you leave behind. Without instructions to the contrary, the state laws of succession will determine who gets your possessions, who raises your children, how your assets will be divided, and who your executor/executrix will be.

In addition, dying intestate gives tacit approval for your relatives to haggle over your belongings (at your expense) *and* over your children, who might become very attractive if they are attached to a large insurance policy naming them as principal beneficiaries.

A well-thought-out will, while not a simplistic solution to all estate-planning issues, can provide a fair and equitable distribution of assets, establish a limitation on estate creditors, and help you distribute your property to those you want to reward.

The bad news is that a will might not accomplish these ends cheaply or expediently. What's more, wills can be contested. A will can serve as a catchall for assets not otherwise directed. Have your will reviewed any time your personal life, your financial circumstances or your health change.

Keep your will and other important documents stored safely in a fireproof box at home near an outside exit. Bank safety deposit boxes can be locked up after a death, and an attorney's office can lose or misplace documents.

Wanted: deed or alive

If you have children from a previous marriage or other heirs to whom you want your real property left, you might want a *warranty deed.* Some states follow a common law basis for directing property, while others view assets owned by either spouse as community property. A spouse might also have a *dower's right* (some right of ownership) in your real estate no matter how you prefer it directed after your death. Consult your legal advisor before making final decisions.

If you own property outside of the state in which you reside, you might encounter more complex estate planning. Some states rule that outside assets pass according to the state in which you reside, while others dictate that the location of the real property determines the estate format.

Trust me on this

Trust-mania is rampant, with gangs of lawyers trying to cash in. But unless your name is Walton or Perot, carefully consider why you need a trust when there are so many other ways to direct your personal property and real estate outside of probate.

A trust document represents a major change in the control of your assets after your death. By establishing a trust, you might be "protecting" your family from your assets instead of providing a fail-safe method of avoiding probate. What's more, trusts become irrevocable at your death and can be so inflexible that they might actually create the very limitations you are seeking to avoid.

If you do establish a trust or make other custodual declarations, think twice before naming a banking institution as the trustee. What if the institution becomes insolvent? What if the bank merges with another after your death? What if the trust officer you've chosen is promoted somewhere else?

'Tis better to gift

Gifting during your lifetime or simple will substitutes are the easiest ways to disburse your property (unless you have a specific problem that demands more complicated estate planning, such as a disabled family member, a spendthrift relative, business interests, or an heir who must be protected). Otherwise, you could be attempting to kill a fly (probate) with a sledgehammer (trust).

All estate-planning solutions require weighing the benefits and disadvantages before deciding how to transfer your property to your loved ones. Perhaps the most dangerous of all is "default" estate planning—doing nothing and letting your survivors battle it out.

To make record-gathering easier for your heirs, executor or executrix, use the handy organizer I've included on the following pages.

Estate Organizer

Important Names/Phone Numbers

Relatives: _____

_____

_____

Employer: _____

Attorney(s): _____

_____

Insurance Agent(s): _____

_____

_____

_____

Financial Planner: _____

_____

Accountant: _____

_____

Other: _____

_____

_____

_____

_____

Doctor's Names & Addresses

Doctor(s): _____

_____

_____

_____

_____

Dentist: _____

_____

Location of Personal Papers

Will: _____

Power of Attorney: _____

Trust(s): _____

_____

Birth/Baptismal Certificate: _____

Marriage Certificate: _____

Military Records: _____

_____

Social Security Card/No.: _____

Other: _____

_____

_____

Insurance Policies (company & location)

Property: _____

_____

_____

Auto: _____

_____

Death (Life): _____

_____

_____

Health: _____

_____

_____

Disability: _____

_____

Medigap Health: _____

Long Term Care: _____

Commercial: _____

_____

_____

_____

_____

Location of Titles

Primary residence: _____

Rental real estate: _____

_____

_____

Car(s): _____

_____

_____

Mortgage: _____

Title insurance: _____

Property deed: _____

Safety deposit box location: _____

_____

Income tax returns location: _____

_____

Any other papers or documents: _____

_____

_____

_____

_____

_____

Chapter Eight

It Ain't Over 'Til It's Over: Managing Your Retirement

Living off your investments, the interest they produce, Social Security and pension checks is a tough row for many retirees to hoe. The grandmother of a friend of mine put it best when she stitched the following quaint needlepoint onto a pillow: Retirement—Half as much money. Twice as much husband.

Most importantly, you must consider the assets you've been banking for your retirement as your "marathon money" and keep it working hard in long-term, inflation-fighting investments.

The most dangerous mistake new retirees can make is to gather their assets around them like a cloak, hanging on to them as if they had less than six months to live. No matter how old you are, you always need a plan for accumulating wealth. You just may live to outspend all of it.

Is it time to retire?

Have you been dreaming of your retirement lifestyle? Well, no matter how wonderful the imagery, you are not ready to retire until you have your investment house in order.

Review the following checklist to determine your retirement readiness:

_____ I know how much my company pension retirement benefits will be.

_____ I have recently sent for a Social Security earnings estimate.

_____ I have completed a current budget to determine my monthly income and expenses.

_____ I am faithfully contributing to my IRA account *even if I can't deduct any of the contributions.*

_____ I know who will pay my medical expenses before and after Medicare kicks in.

_____ I am making plans to keep pace with increasing living costs.

_____ I have a current will.

_____ I have completed a simple estate plan, including a durable power of attorney and a medical living will (if appropriate in your state).

_____ I have a net worth statement (including my real estate and other personal property).

_____ I have discussed finances with my spouse (or other family members) in case I should become ill or pass on.

_____ I have a positive attitude about planning for the future.

_____ I have a backup plan if my company pension or health care programs become insolvent.

_____ I have reviewed my death (life) insurance to determine how much I should have during retirement.

_____ I am planning elective medical, dental or other health care procedures while I still have my company insurance benefits.

_____ My homeowner and auto liability insurance coverage is adequate to protect my retirement assets and other property.

_____ All property deeds and ownership documents are appropriately titled.

_____ I will use retirement to pursue positive personal goals, not as an excuse to revert to a couch potato.

_____ I am getting a financial education to maximize my money before I need to spend it.

_____ I am preparing for inflation before I retire.

_____ I will compare all retirement pension choices before picking a particular option.

_____ I will turn any fear or lack of confidence regarding managing my assets into empowerment through knowledge.

_____ I will put myself, not others, in charge of my financial decisions.

_____ I consider tax planning a last priority for retirement investing, not a primary objective.

_____ I am ignoring sales presentations and investigating my own investment options.

_____ I will not totally depend on any social insurance programs to take care of my retirement needs.

_____ I am subordinating spending in favor of current savings goals.

_____ I understand there are no completely safe investments.

Creating retirement wealth

Successful money management and basic investing haven't changed much in the past 50 years. There are still three rules to adhere to:

>   1. Diversify!
>
>   2. Diversify!
>
>   3. Diversify!

Always choose your priorities before taking action on which direction or investment opportunity to use for your wealth accumulation. You must first consider how the money will be used, the investment vehicle that suits that purpose, and, last and certainly least, tax advantages that can make those investment vehicles even more effective.

Bulls, bears and pigs

Bulls (who think the market is heading up) make money. Bears (who think the opposite) can turn a profit during bad times. But pigs (who are just greedy) usually get slaughtered.

Here are the rules that the smartest animals in the barnyard live by:

1. Always purchase quality investment instruments. Don't speculate.

2. Never invest out of greed or fear. Structure your portfolio for comfort, not for speed.

3. Invest for the long-term. Smooth out your investment highway. Stick to base hits instead of batting for the fences.

4. Diversify your portfolio, no mater how good one product looks.

5. Risk is everywhere—diversify even your *types* of risk.

6. Invest short-term funds in guaranteed investment vehicles.

7. Keep your long-term assets in vehicles that outpace inflation.

8. Watch over your own investment capital.

9. Manage your money yourself, rather than making others rich by doing it for you.

10. Beware of investments that tout tax purposes first.

11. Read the fine print *first*.

12. Make annual IRA contributions, even if you can't deduct them.

I also strongly advise you *not* to choose the most popular investment vehicles and to avoid outmoded traditions. Too many folks purchase financial products for the wrong reasons, without understanding their contracts, thus putting their savings at greater risk than necessary.

Instead, keep a firm grasp on the basic rules of the Money Game—the time value of money, the wonders of compound interest and the *proper* uses of tax-advantaged shelters. Believing unrealistic projections for financial returns will undermine wise common-sense judgments.

Tax angles such as 401ks, IRAs, SEPs, SARSEPs, KEOGHs and TSAs are more powerful with the right investment underneath. Resist the temptation to allow the tax tail to wag the investment dog.

The best way to go: mutual funds

For most retirees, mutual funds are the best way to both build their initial retirement fund and to keep their money outpacing inflation after they've retired. Mutual funds allow you to track your money daily, to get away from the use of financial middlemen, and, therefore, to receive a greater share of the earnings.

The most vital benefit of investing through the mutual fund system, however, is the ability it gives you to create a millionaire's portfolio, no matter *how* small your savings. By placing your retirement nest egg into many baskets and various types of vehicles, you can shelter your precious dollars from specific market anomalies and travel a smoother financial highway.

One of the my other books in this series—**MONEY POWER Through Mutual Funds**—thoroughly discusses everything you would ever want to know about these investment vehicles. While I don't discuss any specific funds, you will quickly figure out what I do recommend: Equity income funds, the "turtles" of the mutual fund arena, are dull, boring and stodgy, yet they slowly win the race against inflation.

If you are retired and need a supplemental income, mutual funds can help. Funds have a variety of withdrawal options. You can request dividends, monthly interest and/or capital gains sent to you instead of being reinvested back into your account. If you have more than one type of fund, you may want a portion from each fund sent to you on a regular basis.

You can even arrange to have a specific dollar amount sent to your address or to your banking institution at monthly intervals. This way, your payment can be directly deposited into your checking account and be conveniently available for immediate spending.

If you need additional money (or less than originally requested) call your fund and request an adjustment. This can usually be processed by the following month.

If you are withdrawing from an IRA account, your fund may request written notice. At all times, IRA rules supersede any mutual fund policies. Your fund's Shareholder Services Department can give you their particular redemption policies.

If you are younger than age 59 1/2 but need a monthly income now, you may be eligible for early withdrawals from your IRA account without incurring a 10% penalty. You must provide your fund with written notice and determine how much can be redeemed under the law which allows this benefit. This easy withdrawal provision allows an IRA owner under age 59 1/2 to take substantially equal payments without penalty (*not* without income taxes) based on his or her future life expectancy.

Once started, the withdrawals must last until age 59 1/2 or five years, whichever is longer. After age 59 1/2 or five years, there are no penalties on withdrawals, just income taxes on pre-tax dollars and the earnings you withdraw. Before you choose any early withdrawal option, consult your tax advisor. Accurate figures are critical, as withdrawing too much or too little can trigger negative tax implications.

If you don't need regular income but do need to tap into your savings occasionally, don't request a withdrawal option. Money you don't currently use will languish if stored in today's embalmed savings accounts. Allow your funds to compound as long as possible before requesting them. Most mutual funds allow telephone redemptions (liquidations) with checks posted the following day and sent to your address of record. In the corporate world, this is called "just in time" delivery: You want your money delivered to you "just in time" for your spending purposes.

Perhaps you need more income than your specific mutual fund throws off in distributions. If you are investing for some growth of principal, you can request the annual accumulations without dipping into your investment principal. If that is insufficient, tighten your budget a bit and request just a little more in your monthly check, even though you may start cutting into investment principal.

Retirees dread this because this is seed money that will never again compound. If they dip into principal long enough, their savings will eventually be wiped out.

To avoid this, too many elderly search for financial products advertising higher yields. Be careful: Higher returns often signal increased risk to investment principal. A better compromise is to stay with more solid, diversified investments and conserve spending.

Leave your IRA accounts intact, if possible, until you turn 70 1/2, when IRS law states you must begin annual withdrawals according to the number of years you are expected to live. This number rarely coincides with your plans. So when you spend IRA accounts that defer taxation, you are depleting the most valuable dollars you own. Use interest from bank CDs first, then general investment accounts, before dipping into IRA funds.

Keep your financial bicycle mechanically sound by rebalancing your asset allocation every couple of years. Don't totally eliminate bank CDs just because higher returns can be gained in a mutual fund account. You always need some tires (bank deposits) on your bicycle. They are the foundation of your investment pyramid.

Keep your IRA statements for the rest of your life, or eternity, whichever comes first. Most mutual funds provide a year-end statement reflecting all activities. In addition, many send cost basis records so you can calculate (for tax purposes) which shares you sold and how much they originally cost.

No matter how old you become, an IRA will be a part of your financial life. If the IRS should ever doubt your reporting, the burden of proof is on your shoulders to explain and clarify. There are significant penalties and painful tax consequences if you cannot show where your IRA accounts have moved and other important data.

If you own a combination of tax-deductible IRA accounts and partially or totally non-deductible IRAs, don't depend on your memory and any institution's records to keep track. A bird in hand is safer than two overhead.

You're now hopefully more informed, charted and budgeted than you ever thought possible...or ever thought you'd want to be. Just in case you haven't had enough, there are a couple more charts and checklists at the end of this chapter.

All told, the information in this book should enable you to win the most important race of your life—the race to keep your money alive as long as you are. So if you haven't done a budget for your planning, if you haven't completed a post-retirement budget, if you haven't organized your estate and, most importantly, if you haven't made sure your current plans will *allow* you to retire, get that calculator back out and crunch some numbers.

Remember: Whether you're a lion or gazelle, you'd better start running!

What Are You Worth?

Liquid Assets

Checking accounts $ _____

Savings accounts $ _____

Money market funds $ _____

Life insurance cash values $ _____

Total Liquid Assets (a) $ _____

Investment Assets

Stocks $ _____

Bonds $ _____

Mutual Funds $ _____

Certificates of Deposit $ _____

Other $ _____

Retirement Plans

IRAs $ _____

401k, 403b, TDA, TSA $ _____

Basic Company Pension $ _____

Other Retirement Plans $ _____

Total Investment Assets (b) $ _____

Personal Assets

Residence $_____

Vacation home or land $_____

Cars $_____

Jewelry/art/antiques $_____

Collections $_____

Other $_____

Total Personal Assets (c) $_____

Total Assets (a + b + c) $_____

Liabilities

Credit card balances $_____

Mortgage $_____

Car loans $_____

Time/personal loan installments $_____

Education loans $_____

Home equity loans $_____

Other $_____

Total Liabilities $_____

Your Net Worth

Total Assets $_____

Minus Total Liabilities $_____

Your Personal Net Worth $_____

Current Status of Financial Goals & Objectives

Date _____

	Completed	Not Completed
Statement of Financial Position	_____	_____
Debt Management Strategies	_____	_____
Emergency Fund Liquidity	_____	_____
Short-term Financial Goals	_____	_____

Risk Management

	Completed	Not Completed
Homeowner Insurance	_____	_____
Auto Insurance	_____	_____
Death (Life) Insurance	_____	_____
Business Liability	_____	_____
Disability	_____	_____
Major Medical Health	_____	_____
Supplemental Health	_____	_____
Nursing Home (Long-term Care)	_____	_____

Estate Planning

	Completed	Not Completed
Current Existing Will	_____	_____
Durable Power of Attorney	_____	_____
Living Will	_____	_____
Trusts	_____	_____
Special Considerations	_____	_____
Property Deed Ownership Form	_____	_____

Total Compensation Benefits

1. Group Basic Term Life Insurance   ❑ YES ❑ NO
   Amount _____

2. Optional Term or other Life Insurance   ❑ YES ❑ NO
   Amount _____

3. Deferred Compensation   ❑ YES ❑ NO
   Amount _____

4. Retirement Health Plan   ❑ YES ❑ NO
   Amount _____

5. Retirement Insurance Plan   ❑ YES ❑ NO
   Amount _____

6. Supplementary Retirement Savings   ❑ YES ❑ NO

   Employer Match _____%   ❑ YES ❑ NO

   Lump Sum Retirement Option   ❑ YES ❑ NO
   (Such as 401k, ESOP, 403b, TSA)

7. Thrift Savings Plan   ❑ YES ❑ NO

   Employer Match _____%   ❑ YES ❑ NO

8. Spouse Health Retirement Plan   ❑ YES ❑ NO

9. Special Considerations   ❑ YES ❑ NO

Types of Survivor Elections

1. Lump Sum Pension Payment   ❑ YES ❑ NO

2. Yourself Only Life Monthly Annuity   ❑ YES ❑ NO

3. Former Spouse Survivor Annuity   ❑ YES ❑ NO

4. Yourself/Spouse Survivor Annuity   ❑ YES ❑ NO

5. Combination Current/Former Spouse   ❑ YES ❑ NO

6. Special Pension Alternatives   ❑ YES ❑ NO

7. Social Security Combination   ❑ YES ❑ NO

Your Retirement Planning Checklist

1. Determine when you are eligible to retire.
2. Identify the factors that affect your pension computation.
3. Make a decision regarding the survivor election (different options available such as a lump sum, life income for you only, or life income for both you and your spouse).
4. Make decisions regarding health and death insurance.
5. Determine your Social Security benefits. (Send in a request for earnings now to compare benefits with my tables and to check the accuracy of all earnings credits.)
6. Estimate your monthly retirement needs.
7. Determine the monthly retirement income needed.
8. Analyze your supplemental retirement savings plans.
9. Adjust your investment vehicles for comfort, not for speed.
10. Determine the monthly income shortfall (gap).
11. Calculate the annual savings necessary.
12. Apply for Social Security benefits three months before eligible.
13. Apply for Medicare Part A three months before age 65.
14. Evaluate whether to enroll in Medicare Part B.
15. Follow additional steps to prepare for and insure a comfortable retirement.

Index

MONEY
POWER
For
Retirement